Sun

Solar Statistics:

- Size: 109.2 times larger than our Earth
- Date of Discovery: Unknown
- Discovered by: Ancient ancestors
- Equatorial Inclination: 7.25 with respect to the ecliptic
- Equatorial Radius: 432,168.6 mi/695,508km
- Equatorial Circumference: 2,715,395.6 mi/4,370,005.6km
- Volume: 338,102,469,632,763,000miles3/ /1,409,272,569,059,860,000km3
- Density: 1.409g/cm3
- Mass: 1,989,100,000,000,000,000,000,000,000,000 kg
- Surface Area: 2,347,017,636,988square mi/6,078,747,774,547km2
- Surface Gravity: 899.0ft/s2/274.0m/s2
- Escape Velocity: 1,381.756 mi/2,223,720km/h

Solar System

Jupiter

Uranus

Saturn

Neptune

Our solar system comprises of eight planets which all circle around our home star, the Sun. " Mercury, Venus, Earth, Mars, Jupiter, Saturn, Uranus and Neptune"

I'm MERCURY

The Smallest Planet →

Mercury Statistics:

- Moons: None
- Distance from Sun: 35.98 million mi
- Radius: 1,516 mi
- Diameter: 4,879 km
- Orbital period: 88 days
- Mass: 3.285 × 10^23 kg (0.055 M⊕)
- Surface Temperature: -173 to 427°C
- Number of Moons: None
- First Record: 14th century BCE by Assyrian astronomers

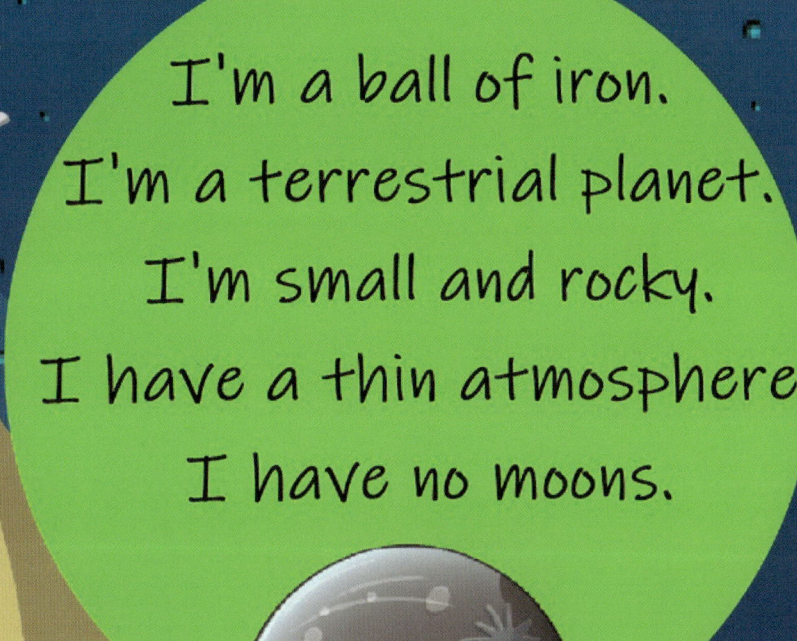

I'm a ball of iron.
I'm a terrestrial planet.
I'm small and rocky.
I have a thin atmosphere
I have no moons.

I'm MERCURY

I am the smallest planet in our solar system
I'm the closest planet to the Sun.

I'm VENUS

the hottest planet

Venus Statistics:

- Distance from Sun: 67.24 million mi
- Radius: 3,760 mi
- Diameter: 7,520.8 mi
- Orbital period: 225 days
- Mass: 4.867 × 10^24 kg 0.815 M⊕
- Surface Temperature: 462 °C
- Number of Moons: None
- First Recorded: 17th century BCE by Babylon astronomers

I am the hottest planet in our solar system.

I'm the same size as the Earth but I spin the other way and much more slowly.

I'm VENUS

I am a terrestrial planet.

I am small and rocky.

I have a thick atmosphere, it traps heat and makes me very hot.

I have an active surface, including volcanoes!

I have no water

I'm the Earth

The Place Where We All Live

Earth Statistics:

- Population: 7.53 billion (2017) Trending, World Bank
- Distance from Sun: 92.96 million mi
- Radius: 3,959 mi
- Polar Diameter: 12,714 km
- Orbital Period: 265.24 days
- Mass: 5.972×10^{24} kg
- Number of Moons: 1
- Age: 4.543 billion years

I am the only known planet in the solar system
that contains free atmospheric oxygen,
the largest amount of liquid water and life.
I am one of the four rocky
or terrestrial planets of the solar system
(the other three are Mercury,
Venus and Mars),
of which I am the largest.
In the solar system,
I am the densest of all
the other planets
I have a moon

I'm the Earth

I am the third planet in the solar
system orbiting the sun.
With a diameter of
about 8,000 miles,
I am the fifth largest
planet in the solar system.

I'm MARS

I am a cold desert world

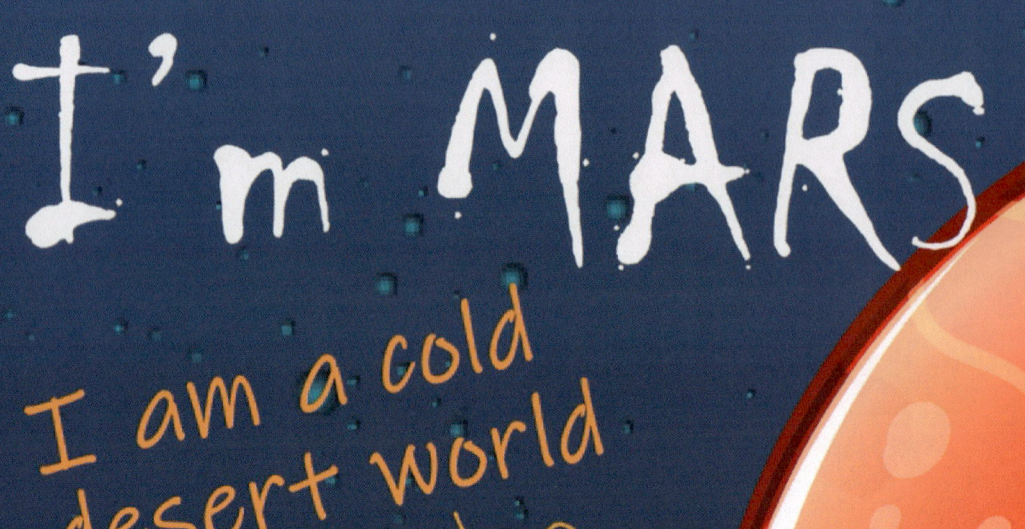

Mars Statistics:

- Distance from Sun: 141.6 million mi
- Radius: 2,106 mi
- Polar Diameter: 6,752 km
- Orbital Period: 6.42 x 10^23 kg (10.7% Earth)
- Mass: 6.39 × 10^23 kg 0.107 M⊕
- Surface pressure: -153 to 20 °C
- Moons: (2) Phobos, Deimos
- First Recorded: 2nd Millennium BCE by Egyptian astronomers

I am half the size of the Earth.

I'm sometimes calling the red planet.

I'm red because of the rusty iron in the ground

My mountains are the highest in our solar system

I'm MARS

I have a thin atmosphere.
I have an active atmosphere, but my surface is not active.
I have 2 moons. Their names are Phobos and Deimos

I'm JUPITER

The Biggest Planet

Jupiter Statistics:

- Distance from Sun: 483.8 million mi
- Rings: 4
- Radius: 43,441 mi
- Polar Diameter: 133,709 km
- Orbital period: 12 years
- Mass: 1.90 × 10^27 kg (318 Earths)
- Length of day: 0d 9h 56m
- Surface area: 23.71 billion mi²
- Effective Temperature: -148 °C
- Moons: (79, including (Io, Europa, Ganymede & Callisto)

I am the biggest planet in our solar system.
I'm a gas giant.
I am mainly composed of hydrogen and helium.

I have a very thick atmosphere.

I have rings, but they are very difficult to see.

I have 79 confirmed moons.

I'm JUPITER

I'm SATURN

Rings of ice and dust →

Saturn Statistics:

- Distance from Sun: 890.8 million mi
- Rings: (30 or more – in 7 groups)
- Radius: 36,184 mi
- Polar Diameter: 108,728 km
- Orbital period: 29 years
- Mass: 5.68×10^{26} kg (95 Earths)
- Length of day: 0d 10h 42m
- Surface area: 16.49 billion mi²
- Moons: (62 including Titan, Enceladus, Iapetus & Rhea)
- First Recorded: 8th Century BCE by the Assyrians

I'm SATURN

I have 53 moons!
I also have nine
unconfirmed moons
Titan is my biggest moon.

I'm a gas giant like Jupiter.
I have a thick atmosphere.
My rings are made of ice.
I'm made mostly of
hydrogen and helium.
I have a lovely set of
seven main rings
with spaces between them.

I'm URANUS

I have 27 moons

Uranus Statistics:

- Distance from Sun: 1.784 billion mi
- Rings: 13
- Radius: 15,759 mi
- Polar Diameter: 49,946 km
- Orbital period: 84 years
- Mass: 8.68 × 10^25 kg (15 Earths)
- Effective Temperature: -216 °C
- Moons: (27, including Miranda, Titania, Ariel, Umbriel & Oberon)
- Date of Discovery: March 13, 1781 by William Herschel

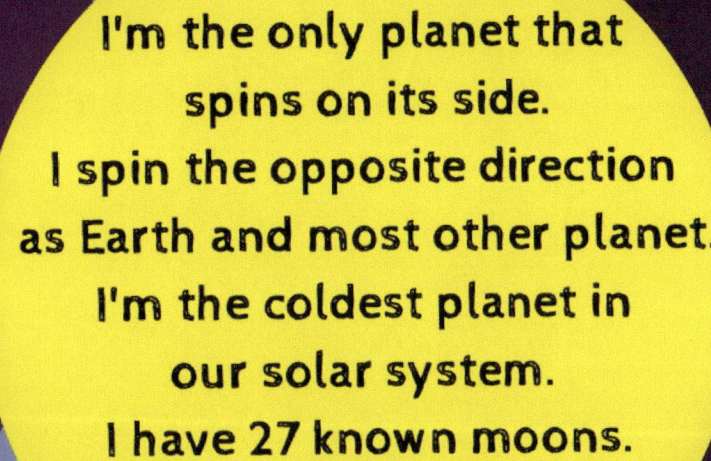

I'm the only planet that spins on its side.
I spin the opposite direction as Earth and most other planet.
I'm the coldest planet in our solar system.
I have 27 known moons.

I'm URANUS

I'm surrounded by a set of 13 rings.
I'm an ice giant
(instead of a gas giant).
I'm mostly made of flowing icy materials above a solid core.
I have a thick atmosphere made of methane, hydrogen, and helium.

I'm NEPTUNE

I'm the farthest planet from the sun

Neptune Statistics:

- Distance from Sun: 2.793 billion mi
- Rings: 5
- Radius: 15,299 mi
- Polar Diameter: 48,682 km
- Orbital period: 165 years
- Mass: 1.024 × 10^26 kg (17.15 M⊕)
- Moons: (14, including Triton)
- Date of Discovery: September 23, 1846 by Urbain Le Verrier & Johann Galle

I am surrounded by six rings.
I am made of a thick soup of water, ammonia and methane flowing over a solid core the size of Earth.

I'm NEPTUNE

I have a thick and windy atmosphere.
I'm an icy gas giant.
I'm the farthest planet from the sun.
I have many storms.
I have 13 moons (and one more awaiting confirmation of discovery).

Printed in Great Britain
by Amazon